Peace Pilgrim

In Her Own Words

"If you realized how powerful your thoughts are, you would never think a negative thought."

"Constantly through thought you are creating your inner conditions and helping to create the conditions around you. So keep your thoughts on the positive side, think about the best that could happen, think about the good things you want to happen."

"If only you could see the whole picture, if you knew the whole story, you would realize that no problem ever comes to you that does not have a purpose in your life, that cannot contribute to your inner growth. When you perceive this, you will recognize that problems are opportunities in disguise. If you did not face problems, you would just drift through life. It is through solving problems in accordance with the highest light we have that inner growth is attained."

"If you are harboring the slightest bitterness toward anyone, or any unkind thoughts of any sort whatever, you must get rid of them quickly. They are not hurting anyone but you. It isn't enough just to do right things and say right things - you must also think right things before your life can come into harmony."

"Life is like a mirror. Smile at it and it smiles back at you."

"Do you know God? Do you know there is a power greater than ourselves which manifests itself within us as well as everywhere else in the universe? This I call God. Do you know what it is to know God, to have God's constant guidance, a constant awareness of God's presence? To know God is to reflect love toward all people and all creations. To know God is to feel peace within - a calmness, a serenity, an unshakeableness which enables you to face any situation. To know God is to be so filled with joy that it bubbles over and goes forth to bless the world."

"For those of you who are seeing the spiritual life, I recommend these four daily practices: Spend time alone each day in receptive silence. When angry, or afflicted with any negative emotion, take time to be alone with God. (Do not talk with people who are angry; they are irrational and cannot be reasoned with. If you or they are angry, it is best to leave and pray.) Visualize God's light each day and send it to someone who needs help. Exercise the body, it is the temple of the soul."

"The way of peace is the way of love. Love is the greatest power on earth. It conquers all things."

"I am constantly thankful. The world is so beautiful, I am thankful. I have endless energy, I am thankful. I am plugged into the source of Universal Supply, I am thankful. I am plugged into the source of Universal Truth, I am thankful. I have this constant feeling of thankfulness, which is a prayer."

"Live in the present. Do the things that need to be done. Do all the good you can each day. The future will unfold"

"I have chosen the positive approach - instead of stressing the bad things which I am against, I stress the good things which I am for."

"Overcome evil with good, falsehood with truth, and hatred with love. The message isn't new, but we haven't learned to live it yet."

"I no longer become angry. I not only do not say angry words, I do not even think angry thoughts! If someone does an unkind thing to me I feel only compassion instead of resentment. Even upon those who cause suffering I look with deep compassion, knowing the harvest of sorrow that lies in store for them. If there were those who hated me, I would love them in return, knowing that hatred can only be overcome by love, and knowing that there is good in all human beings which can be reached by a loving approach."

"Never think of any right effort as being fruitless. All right effort bears fruit, whether we see the results or not."

"Praying without ceasing is not ritualized, nor are there even words. It is a constant state of awareness of oneness with God."

"There is great freedom in simplicity of living."

"The pain and suffering that comes to us has a purpose in our lives-it is trying to teach us something. We should look for its lesson."

"Worry is a useless mulling over of things we cannot change."

"When love fills your life all limitations are gone. The medicine this sick world needs so badly is love."

"After you have found inner peace you have endless energy - the more you give, the more you receive. After you have found your calling, you work easily and joyously. You never get tired."

"What we usually call human evolution is the awakening of the divine nature within us."

"Unnecessary possessions are unnecessary burdens. If you have them, you have to take care of them! There is great freedom in simplicity of living. It is those who have enough but not too much who are the happiest."

"There is a criterion by which you can judge whether the thoughts you are thinking and the things you are doing are right for you. The criterion is: Have they brought you inner peace?"

"Do not believe in me or any other teacher, rather trust in your own inner voice. This is your guide, this is your teacher. Your teacher is within not without. Know yourself, not me!"

"Intellectually I touched God many times as truth and emotionally I touched God as love. I touched God as goodness. I touched God as kindness. It came to me that God is a creative force, a motivating power, an over-all intelligence, an ever-present, all pervading spirit - which binds everything in the universe together and gives life to everything. That brought God close. I could not be where God is not. You are within God. God is within you."

"Anything you cannot relinquish when it has outlived its usefulness possesses you, and in this materialistic age a great many of us are possessed by our possessions."

"The simplification of life is one of the steps to inner peace. A persistent simplification will create an inner and outer well-being that places harmony in one's life."

"No one can find inner peace except by working, not in a self-centered way, but for the whole human family."

"The path of the seeker is full of pitfalls and temptations, and the seeker must walk it alone with God. I would recommend that you keep your feet on the ground and your thoughts at lofty heights, so that you may attract only good. Concentrate on giving so that you may open yourself to receiving; concentrate on living according to the light you have so that you may open yourself to more light; get as much light as possible through the inner way."

"You can visualize God's light each day and send it to someone who needs help. Your divine nature must reach out and touch the divine nature of another. Within you is the light of the world, it must be shared with the world."

"There is something to that old saying that hate injures the hater, not the hated."

"A few really dedicated people can offset the masses of out of harmony people, so we who work for peace must not falter, we must continue to pray for peace and to act for peace in whatever way we can. We must continue to speak for peace and to live the way of peace; to inspire others, we must continue to think of peace and know that peace is possible. What we dwell upon we help bring to manifestation. One little person giving all of her time to peace makes news. Many people giving some of their time can make history."

"Know that you are God's beautiful child, always in God's hands. Accept God... accept God's protection... there is really no problem to fear. Know that you are not the clay garment. Know that you are not the self-centered nature which governs your life needlessly. Know that you are the God-centered nature, The Kingdom of God within. The Indwelling Christ. Eternal and indestructible. Identify with the real you."

"Visualize a golden light within you and spread it out. First to those about you - your circle of friends and relatives - and then gradually to the world. Keep on visualizing God's golden light surrounding our earth."

"When you perceive that problems serve a purpose in your life, you will recognize that problems are opportunities in disguise."

"There is no glimpse of the light without walking the path. You can't get it from anyone else, nor can you give it to anyone. Just take whatever steps seem easiest for you, and as you take a few steps it will be easier for you to take a few more."

"The fear habit is very detrimental because you attract the things you fear. If we have any fear we need to get rid of it."

"Do not suppress it - that would hurt you inside. Do not express it - this would not only hurt you inside, it would cause ripples in your surroundings. What you do is transform it."

"If you recognize that all of your inner hurts are caused by your own wrong actions or your own wrong reactions or your own wrong inaction, then you will stop hurting yourself."

"We are all cells in the body of humanity - all of us, all over the world. Each one has a contribution to make, and will know from within what this contribution is."

"The world is like a mirror; if you smile at it, it smiles at you. I love to smile, and so in general, I definitely receive smiles in return."

"Pure love is a willingness to give without a thought of receiving anything in return."

"Live according to your highest light and more light will be given."

"Humanity can only improve as people improve. When you have improved your life, you can inspire those around you to want to improve their lives. Remember that a few in harmony with God's will are more powerful than multitudes out of harmony."

"A life without problems would be a barren existence, without the opportunity for spiritual growth."

"Prayer is a concentration of positive thoughts."

"When you make people angry, they act in accordance with their baser instincts, often violently and irrationally. When you inspire people, they act in accordance with their higher instincts, sensibly and rationally. Also, anger is transient, whereas inspiration sometimes has a life-long effect."

"You must give if you want to receive. Let the center of your being be one of giving, giving, giving. You can't give too much, and you will discover you cannot give without receiving."

"Walk with me, but don't follow me blindly. Hold fast to the truth, not to my garments. My body is merely a clay structure; today it is here, tomorrow it shall be gone. If you attach yourself to me today, what are you going to do tomorrow when I am not with you? Attach yourself to God, attach yourself to humanity, only then will you be closer to me."

"You must learn to forgive yourself as easily as you forgive others. And then take a further step and use all that energy that you used in condemning yourself for improving yourself. After that I really started to get somewhere - because there's only one person you can change and that's yourself. After you have changed yourself, you might be able to inspire others to look for change."

"You have much more power when you are working for the right thing than when you are working against the wrong thing. And, of course, if the right thing is established wrong things will fade away of their own accord."

"At a simple level, good is that which helps people-evil is that which hurts people. At a higher level, good is that which is in harmony with divine purpose-evil is that which is out of harmony with divine purpose."

"People allow themselves to be slaves of their bad habits and society's bad habits - but they have free will, and if they wish to be free they can."

"There is a spark of good in everybody, no matter how deeply it may be buried. It is the real you."

"For light I go directly to the Source of light, not to any of the reflections."

"People have found inner peace by losing themselves in a cause larger than themselves. Finding inner peace means coming from the self-centered life into the life centered."

"Collective problems must be solved by all of us, collectively, and no one finds inner peace who avoids doing his or her share in the solving of collective problems."

"My appointed work is to awaken the divine nature that is within."

"Fountain of Love my source is in thee - Loving thy will my spirit is free - Beautiful day when all of us see - The hope of the world is Love!"

"When you feel the need for a spiritual lift, try getting to bed early and get up early to have a quiet time at dawn. Then carry the serene 'in tune' feeling that comes to you into your day, no matter what you may be doing."

"We must be able to appreciate and enjoy the places where we tarry and yet pass on without anguish when we are called elsewhere. In our spiritual development we are often required to pull up roots many times and to close many chapters in our lives until we are no longer attached to any material thing and can love all people without any attachment to them."

"It isn't enough just to do right things and say right things, you must also think right things before your life can come into harmony."

"Any praise I receive does not change me, for I pass it right along to God. I walk because God gives me strength to walk, I live because God gives me the supply to live, I speak because God gives me the words to speak. All I did was to surrender my will to God's will. My entire life has prepared me for this undertaking. This is my calling. This is my vocation. This is what I must be doing. I could not be happy doing anything else."

"We people of the world need to find ways to get to know one another - for then we will recognize that our likenesses are so much greater than our differences, however great our differences may seem. Every cell, every human being, is of equal importance and has work to do in this world"

"Although others may feel sorry for you, never feel sorry for yourself: it has a deadly effect on spiritual well-being. Recognize all problems, no matter how difficult, as opportunities for spiritual growth, and make the most of these opportunities."

"People have had to make up for their spiritual impoverishment by accumulating material things. When spiritual blessings come, material blessings seem unimportant. As long as we desire material things this is all we receive, and we remain spiritually impoverished."

"It is not through judgment that the good in people can be reached, but through love and faith."

"Pure love is a willingness to give, without a thought of receiving anything in return. Love can save the world from. Love God: turn to God with receptiveness and responsiveness. Love your fellow human beings: turn to them with friendliness and givingness. Make yourself fit to be called a child of God by living the way of love."

"If you want to serve the universe, the obvious place to begin is right where you are. That's where I began. I looked at every situation I came into and wondered, 'What can I do to be of service in this situation?' Sometimes there was nothing I could do, but often there was - a helping hand, a word of cheer, a pleasant smile. Then, after I had given a lot, a most wonderful spiritual receiving began - giving me more to give."

"As I lived up to the highest light I had, higher and higher light came to me."

"The simplification of life is one of the steps to inner peace."

"If only you could see the whole picture, if you knew the whole story, you would realize that no problem ever comes to you that does not have a purpose in your life, that cannot contribute to your inner growth."

"Just concentrate on thinking and living and acting in harmony with God's laws and inspiring others to do likewise."

"Anything you strive to hold captive will hold you captive, and if you desire freedom you must give freedom."

"I am a deeply religious person, but I belong to no denomination. I follow the spirit of God's law, not the letter of the law. One can become so attached to the outward symbols and structure of religion that one forgets its original intent - to bring one closer to God. We can only gain access to the Kingdom of God by realizing it dwells within us as well as in all humanity. Know that we are all cells in the ocean of infinity, each contributing to the others' welfare."

"Most human beings only scratch the surface of their real potential. They have no idea what they're capable of."

"I talk to groups studying the most advanced spiritual teachings and sometimes these people wonder why nothing is happening in their lives. Their motive is the attainment of inner peace for themselves - which of course is a selfish motive. You will not find it with this motive. The motive, if you are to find inner peace, must be an outgoing motive. Service, of course, service. Giving, not getting. Your motive must be good if your work is to have good effect. The secret of life is being of service."

"What I walk on is not the energy of youth, it is a better energy. I walk on the endless energy of inner peace that never runs out! When you become a channel through which God works there are no more limitations, because God does the work through you: you are the instrument - and what God can do is unlimited. When you are working for God you do not find yourself striving and straining. You find yourself calm, serene and unhurried."

"I recognized that there are some well-known, little understood, and seldom practiced laws that we must live by if we wish to find peace within or without. Included are the laws that evil can only be overcome by good; that only good means can attain a good end; that those who do unloving things hurt themselves spiritually."

"Ultimate peace begins within; when we find peace within there will be no more conflict, nor more occasion for war."

"If we fear nothing and radiate love, we can expect good things to come."

"When I started out on my pilgrimage, I was using walking for two purposes at that time. One was to contact people, and I still use it for that purpose today. But the other was as a prayer discipline. To keep me concentrated on my prayer for peace. And after a few years I discovered something. I discovered that I no longer needed the prayer discipline. I pray without ceasing now. My personal prayer is: Make me an instrument through which only truth can speak."

"Of course, I love everyone I meet. How could I fail to! Within everyone is the spark of God. I am not concerned with racial or ethnic background or the color of one's skin; all people look to me like shining lights! I see in all creatures the reflections of God. All people are my kinfolk - people to me are beautiful!"

"No one walks so safely as one who walks humbly and harmlessly with great love and great faith. For such a person gets through to the good in others (and there is good in everyone), and therefore cannot be harmed. This works between individuals, it works between groups and it would work between nations if nations had the courage to try it."

"Just after I dedicated my life to service, I felt that I could no longer accept more than I need while others in the world have less than they need. This moved me to bring my life down to need level. I thought it would be difficult. I thought it would entail a great many hardships, but I was quite wrong. Instead of hardships, I found a wonderful sense of peace and joy, and a conviction that unnecessary possessions are only unnecessary burdens."

"A PILGRIM IS A WANDERER WITH A PURPOSE. A pilgrimage can be to a place - that's the best known kind - but it can also be for a thing. Mine is for peace, and that is why I am a Peace Pilgrim."

"Life is a mixture of successes and failures. May you be encouraged by the successes and strengthened by the failures. As long as you never lose faith in God, you will be victorious over any situation you may face."

"If you realize that those who do mean things are psychologically ill, your feelings of anger will turn to feelings of pity."

"Judging others will avail you nothing and injure you spiritually. Only if you can inspire others to judge themselves will anything worthwhile have been accomplished. When you approach others in judgment they will be on the defensive. When you are able to approach them in a kindly, loving manner without judgment they will tend to judge themselves and be transformed."

"The valid research for the future is on the inner side, on the spiritual side."

"I pray without ceasing now. My personal prayer is: Make me an instrument which only truth can speak."

"You are within God. God is within you."

"Now there is living to give instead of to get. As you concentrate on the giving, you discover that just as you cannot receive without giving, so neither can you give without receiving - even the most wonderful things like health and happiness and inner peace. There is a feeling of endless energy, it just never runs out, it seems to be as endless as air. You seem to be plugged in to the source of universal energy."

"Those who have overcome self-will and become instruments to do God's work can accomplish tasks which are seemingly impossible, but they experience no feeling of self achievement. I now know myself to be a part of the infinite cosmos, not separate from other souls or God. My illusory self is dead; the real self controls the garment of clay and uses it for God's work."

"THIS IS THE WAY OF PEACE: Overcome evil with good, falsehood with truth, and hatred with love... My simple peace message is adequate - really just the message that the way of peace is the way of love. Love is the greatest power on earth. It conquers all things. One in harmony with God's law of love has more strength than an army, for one need not subdue an adversary; an adversary can be transformed."

"If you realized how powerful your thoughts are, you would never think a defeatist or negative thought. Since we create through thought, we need to concentrate very strongly on positive thoughts. If you think you can't do something, you can't. But if you think you can, you may be surprised to discover that you can. It is important that our thoughts be constantly for the best that could happen in a situation - for the good things we would like to see happen."

"You have endless energy only when you are working for the good of the whole - you have to stop working for your little selfish interests. That's the secret of it. In this world you are given as you give."

"How often are you worrying about the present moment? The present moment is usually all right. If you're worrying, you're either agonizing over the past which you should have forgotten long ago, or else you're apprehensive over the future which hasn't even come yet. We tend to skip over the present moment which is the only moment God gives any of us to live."

"When you have done the spiritual growing up you realize that every human being is of equal importance, has work to do in this world, and has equal potential. We are in many varied stages of growth; this is true because we have free will. You have free will as to whether you will finish the mental and emotional growing up. Many choose not to."

"Difficulties with material things often come to remind us that our concentration should be on spiritual things instead of material things. Sometimes difficulties of the body come to show that the body is just a transient garment, and that the reality is the indestructible essence which activates the body. But when we can say, 'Thank God for problems which are sent for our spiritual growth.' They are no longer problems. They then become opportunities."

"It is those who have enough but not too much who are the happiest."

"I don't eat junk foods and I don't think junk thoughts! Let me tell you, junk thoughts can destroy you even more quickly than junk food. Junk thoughts are something to be wary of."

"All who act upon their highest motivations become a power for good. Know that every right thing you do - every good word you say - every positive thought you think - has a good effect."

"We spend a great deal of time telling God what we think should be done, and not enough time waiting in the stillness for God to tell us what to do."

"What people really suffer from is immaturity. Among mature people war would not be a problem - it would be impossible."

"The purpose of problems is to push you toward obedience to God's laws, which are exact and cannot be changed. We have the free will to obey them or disobey them. Obedience will bring harmony, disobedience will bring you more problems... There was a time when I thought it was a nuisance to be confronted with a problem. I tried to get rid of it. I tried to get somebody else to solve it for me. But that was a long time ago. It was a great day in my life when I discovered the wonderful purpose of problems. Yes, they have a wonderful purpose."

"In order to help usher in the golden age we must see the good in people. We must know it is there, no matter how deeply it may be buried. Yes, apathy is there and selfishness is there - but good is there also. It is not through judgment that the good can be reached, but through love and faith."

"In all the people I meet - though some may be governed by the self-centered nature and may not know their potential at all - I see that divine spark. And that's what I concentrate on. All people look beautiful to me; they look like shining lights to me. I always have the feeling of being thankful for these beautiful people who walk the earth with me."

"It does not matter what name you attach to it, but your consciousness must ascend to the point through which you view the universe with your God-centered nature. The feeling accompanying this experience is that of complete oneness with the Universal Whole... This God-centered nature is constantly awaiting to govern your life gloriously. You have the free will to either allow it to govern your life, or not to allow it to affect you. The choice is always yours!"

"It concerns me when I see a small child watching the hero shoot the villain on television. It is teaching the small child to believe that shooting people is heroic. The hero just did it and it was effective. It was acceptable and the hero was well thought of afterward. If enough of us find inner peace to affect the institution of television, the little child will see the hero transform the villain and bring him to a good life. He'll see the hero do something significant to serve fellow human beings. So little children will get the idea that if you want to be a hero you must help people."

"Believing that war is contrary to the will of God and to common sense, and feeling that the way of peace is the way of love, I shall work for peace by using the way of love myself, by helping any group I am part of to use it, by helping the nation of which I am a citizen to use it, by helping the United Nations to use it, and by praying that the way of love be used all over the world."

"You can find God if you will only seek - by obeying divine laws, by loving people, by relinquishing self-will, attachments, negative thoughts and feelings. And when you find God it will be in stillness. You will find God within."

"Then there is the way that was taught two thousand years ago - of overcoming evil with good, which is my way, the way Jesus taught. Never loose faith: God's way is bound to prevail in the end."

"Think about all the good things of your life. Never think about your difficulties. Forget yourself, and concentrate on being of service as much as you can in this world, and then, having lost your lower self in a cause greater than yourself, you will find your higher self: your real self."

"Religion is not an end in itself. One's union with God is the ultimate goal. There are so many religions because immature people tend to emphasize trivial differences instead of important likenesses. Differences between faiths lie in creeds and rituals rather than in religious principles."

"It takes quite a while for the living to catch up with the believing, but of course it can. As we live up to the highest light we have, more light is given."

"Never underestimate the power of a loosely knit group working for a good cause. All of us who work for peace together, all of us who pray for peace together, are a small minority, but a powerful spiritual fellowship. Our power is beyond our numbers."

"Few find inner peace but this is not because they try and fail, it is because they do not try. . . When your life is governed by the divine nature instead of the self-centered nature you have found inner peace."

"Ultimate peace begins within; when we find peace within there will be no more conflict, no more occasion for war. If this is the peace you seek, purify your body by sensible living habits, purify your mind by expelling all negative thoughts, purify your motives by casting out any ideas of greed or self-striving and by seeking to serve you fellow human beings, purify your desires by eliminating all wishes for material possessions or self-glorification and by desiring to know and do God's will for you. Inspire others to do likewise."

"It's very important to get your desires centered so you will desire only to do God's will for you. You can come to the point of oneness of desire, just to know and do your part in the Life Pattern. When you think about it, is there anything else as really important to desire?"

"There is no greater block to world peace or inner peace than fear. What we fear we tend to develop an unreasoning hatred for, so we come to hate and fear. This not only injures us psychologically and aggravates world tension, but through such negative concentration we tend to attract the things we fear. If we fear nothing and radiate love, we can expect good things to come. How much this world needs the message and example of love and of faith!"

"Implanting spiritual ideas in children is very important. Many people live their entire lives according to the concepts that are implanted in them in childhood. When children learn they will get the most attention and love through doing constructive things, they will tend to stop doing destructive things. Most important of all, remember that children learn through example. No matter what you say it is what you do that will have an influence on them."

"When we attempt to isolate another we only isolate ourselves. We are all God's children and there are no favorites. God is revealed to all who seek; God speaks to all who will listen. Be still and know God."

"A few really dedicated people can offset the ill effects of masses of out-of-harmony people, so we who work for peace must not falter."

"The sanctuary of peace dwells within. Seek it out and all things will be added to you. We're coming closer and closer to the time when enough of us will have found inner peace to affect our institutions for the better. And as soon as this happens the institutions will in turn, through example, affect for the better those who are still immature."

"I also made two very important discoveries as time went on. In the first place, I discovered that making money was easy. I had been led to believe that money and possessions would insure me a life of happiness and peace of mind. So that was the path I pursued. In the second place, I discovered that making money and spending it foolishly was completely meaningless. I knew that this was not what I was here for."

"People sometimes ask me if I do not feel lonely on holidays. How can I feel lonely when I live in the constant awareness of God's presence? I love and I enjoy being with people, but when I am alone I enjoy being alone with God."

"Remember that no one can hurt you except yourself. If someone does a mean thing to you, that person is hurt. You are not really hurt unless you become embittered, or unless you become angry and perhaps do a mean thing in return."

"I shall remain a wanderer until mankind has learned the way of peace."

"Religion is not an end in itself. One's union with God is the ultimate goal."

"It is through solving problems correctly that we grow spiritually. We are never given a burden unless we have the capacity to overcome it. If a great problem is set before you, this merely indicates that you have the great inner strength to solve a great problem. There is never really anything to be discouraged about, because difficulties are opportunities for inner growth, and the greater the difficulty the greater the opportunity for growth."

"It is my mission as a pilgrim to act as a messenger expressing spiritual truths. It is a task which I accept joyfully, and I desire nothing in return, neither praise or glory, nor the glitter of silver and gold. I simply rejoice to be able to follow the whisperings of a Higher Will."

"I am never lonely or discouraged or tired. When you live in constant communion with God, you cannot be lonely. When you perceive the working of God's wonderful plan and know that all good effort bears good fruit, you cannot be discouraged. When you have found inner peace, you are in contact with the source of universal energy and cannot be tired."

"The spiritual life is the real life; all else is illusion and deception. Only those who are attached to God alone are truly free. Only those who live up to the highest light live in harmony. All who act upon their highest motivations become a power for good. It is not important that others be noticeably affected: results should never be sought or desired. Know that every right thing you do - every good word you say - every positive thought you think - has good effect."

"We must walk according to the highest light we have, encountering lovingly those who are out of harmony, and trying to inspire them toward a better way. Whenever you bring harmony into any unpeaceful situation, you contribute to the cause of peace. When you do something for world peace, peace among groups, peace among individuals, or your own inner peace, you improve the total peace picture."

"I learned about forty years ago that money and things wouldn't make people happy. And this has been confirmed many times. I have met many millionaires. They had one thing in common. None of them were happy....I realize that if you don't have enough you won't be happy. Neither are you happy if you have too much. It is those who have enough but not too much who are the happiest."

"There is within the hearts of people a deep desire for peace on earth, and they would speak for peace if they were not bound by apathy, by ignorance, by fear. It is the job of the peacemakers to inspire them from their apathy, to dispel their ignorance with truth, to allay their fear with faith that God's laws work - and work for good."

"The simplification of life is one of the steps to inner peace. A persistent simplification will create an inner and outer well-being that places harmony in one's life. For me this began with a discovery of the meaninglessness of possessions beyond my actual and immediate needs. As soon as I had brought myself down to need level, I began to feel a wonderful harmony in my life between inner and outer well-being, between spiritual and material well-being."

"When you have found inner peace, you are in constant contact with the source of universal energy and cannot be tired. . . You have endless energy."

"We have all the light we need, we just need to put it in practice."

"All of us can work for peace. We can work right where we are, right within ourselves, because the more peace we have within our own lives, the more we can reflect into the outer situation."

"I do my work easily and joyously. I feel beauty all around me and I see beauty in everyone I meet, for I see God in everything. I recognize my part in the Life Pattern and I find harmony through gladly and joyously living it. I recognize my oneness with all mankind and my oneness with God. My happiness overflows in loving and giving toward everyone and everything."

Printed in Great Britain
by Amazon

83663978R00088